Measures of Weather

J. R. Carpenter is an artist and writer working across performance, print, and digital media. Her work ask questions about place, displacement, colonialism, and climate. *The Gathering Cloud* (Uniformbooks) won the New Media Writing Prize 2016. *An Ocean of Static* (Penned in the Margins) was commended by the Forward Prizes 2019. *This is a Picture of Wind* (Longbarrow Press) was listed in *The Guardian*'s best poetry books of 2020. *The Pleasure of the Coast* was published by Pamenar Press in 2023. For more information visit luckysoap.com

Also by J.R. Carpenter

The Pleasure of the Coast (Pamenar Press 2023)
City of Marvels (Broken Sleep Books 2023)
This is a Picture of Wind (Longbarrow Press 2020)
Words for Worlds Upended (Guillemot Press 2020)
A General History of the Air (above/ground 2020)
An Ocean of Static (Penned in the Margins 2018)
The Gathering Cloud (Uniformbooks 2017)
GENERATION[S] (Traumawien 2010)
Words the Dog Knows (Conundrum Press 2008)

Measures of Weather

J. R. Carpenter

Shearsman Books

First published in the United Kingdom in 2025 by
Shearsman Books Ltd
PO Box 4239
Swindon
SN3 9FN

Shearsman Books Ltd Registered Office
30–31 St. James Place, Mangotsfield, Bristol BS16 9JB
(this address not for correspondence)

www.shearsman.com

ISBN 978-1-84861-975-3

Copyright © J. R. Carpenter, 2025.

The right of J. R. Carpenter to be identified as the author of this work
has been asserted by her in accordance with the
Copyrights, Designs and Patents Act of 1988.
All rights reserved.

CONTENTS

Of Fire					9
Of a New Comet				11
Of the Moon				17
Of Glass				21
Of Coast				25
Of River				32
Of River Ice				33
Of Watches				34
Of Time					35
Of Swift				40
Of Drip					41
Of Doubles				42
Of Drought				43
Of Lament				49
Of Wind					51
Of Witches				57
Of Dew					65
Of Air					69
Of West					77
Of Where?				87
Of Nothing				93

Of Sources				94
Of Thanks				95

"Days heap upon us. All plain."
—Lisa Robertson, *The Weather*

"We continually miss the mark of the present,
the weather's edge."
—Etel Adnan, *Paris, When It's Naked*

OF FIRE

for Karen Russell

wind whipped snow
at the kitchen window
for all of twenty minutes

then stilled, starlit
we walked into it
night black as Black Angus

we braved the pitch pasture
waved our flashlight shields
caught no eyes, hollow glinting

stepped in no holes, ankle-twisting
stubbed no toes on frozen
earth or dung

from hearthstone to flagstone
we lugged logs, sheltered lighters
skirted smoke, circled flames.

where to look –
down at the near heat
or up at far fire

OF A NEW COMET

after Caroline Hershel

2 August 1786

I venture to trouble you
in absence

with the following
imperfect account

sweeping
in the neighbourhood

of the sun
last night

I found an object
very much resembling

in colour and brightness
the twenty-seventh nebula

with the difference
of being round

a haziness coming on
it was not possible

to satisfy
myself

as to its motion
until this evening

I made several drawings
I have enclosed copies

with my observations annexed
that you may compare them

the star-like
object in the centre

out of focus
while the rest are distinct

makes an isosceles triangle
with the two stars

a and *b*
but so hazy

I cannot sufficiently see
the small star *b*

evident motion
since last night

another
considerable star

c
may be taken

into the field
of view

I cannot find the stars
a and *c*

in any catalogue
but suppose they may be

easily traced
in the heavens

OF THE MOON

after Robert Hooke

of the appearance
of the parts
of the moon

I have observed
by a thirty-foot glass
a spacious vale

encompassed
by a ridge
of hills

not high
in comparison
nor yet steep

the vale itself
is much the figure
of a pear

and seems
a fruitful place
its surface

covered over
with diverse kinds
of vegetables

of the light
it seems to give
a greater reflection

than the more barren tops
of the encompassing hills
of the moon

so that I am not
unapt to think
that the vale

may have vegetables
analogous to our shrubs
and the hills may be covered

with so a thin
a vegetable coat
as the short

sheep pasture
which covers the hills
of Salisbury Plains

this
I confess
is a probability

not a demonstration

OF GLASS

after Margaret Cavendish

of magnifying and multiplying glasses
I have neither studied
nor practiced

that art
with all its instruments
does more easily alter than inform

concave and convex glasses
represent the figure of an object
in no part exactly

a glass that is flawed
or cut into lozenges or squares or the like
will present numerous pictures of one object

the perception of the senses
goes no further than the exterior
of the object presented

that art
for the most part
makes hermaphroditical
      mixed figures
           partly natural
           partly artificial
as pewter
which is between tin and lead

the truth
by art magnified
appears misshapen
      diseased, swollen
      ready, ripe for incision

a louse
by the help of a glass
appears like a lobster

flies will appear
of several forms
      figures

the picture
is not the real
body

mistakes
may easily be committed
in taking copies from copies

if a painter should draw birds
according to colours the microscope presents
what advantage for fowlers?

a high heel to a short leg
is apt to make the wearer fall

an edge
may well seem flat

a point of a needle
a globe

                                                                 by art
                                      the truth of an object
                                      will hardly be known

OF COAST

>   between the ship and the quay
>   lies two metres of incompressible ocean

>   two metres of light between the edge
>   of the sea and the horizon

our labours commence at sun-rise
and do not terminate until night

every precaution is taken
to guard against errors

by calculations I arrive
at the exact number of months

I will have to endure this island
before a ship will be sent to search

already __
—
I am __
—
cramped __
—
by these __
—
small _
—
divisions __
—
of time __

the coast establishes a sort of islet
within common human relation

the months leave their notches on me
the island has no need of me

you want something to happen
and nothing does

what happens to the coast
does not happen to the discourse

like a cork on the waves
I remain motionless

boredom is not far from bliss:
it is bliss seen from the shores of pleasure.

those who have never been afloat
cannot be aware

of the inaccuracies arising
from the slight errors that creep into charts

on a rock that dominates the sea
a metre is divided into centimetres

the Pacific could be measured on it
to within a millimetre

carved in letters
of five centimetres in height

the beginning of a phrase...
I AM

I am the Controller of Weights and Measures

I am not necessarily captivated by the coast of pleasure

I am no longer anything

                                    but an eye

OF RIVER

a ria. a rise
a river runs
green in the shadow
of a steep wooded bank

deep roots tangle in dense strata
the rucked sheets of the Dartmouth beds
the ancient stone of the Lower Devonian
a dark strip between water and leaf

slate slants askance at the falling tide
mist eats green leaves alive
cloud shadows the far shore
counterfeits the coast

the river rolls out its yardage
bolts of shot silk shiver silver
pocked pewter
puckering grey

rain like we haven't seen for some time
stains the parched fields green
pummelled plums fall
purple eggs from the sky

OF RIVER ICE

the sky. lapis. a lapsus.
a slip of warmth. a spell of trees.
a north of wind. shakes the branches.
loose. of the last. of the leaves.

the river. a massive mass. of contradictions.
or maybe dialectics. dialogues between.
frozen and flooded. solid and shattered.
swift and still. silver and silt.

the river ice. never moving. when out walking.
have yet to catch it. cracking / rucking // buckling ///
so when then. does it happen.
this sheering / slicing // piling ///

ice autocorrects to I've on my phone.
I've formed in the river. I've frozen eyelashes.
I've encased slender branches. succumbed in spots.
slicked the path. dripped. in low slung.

sun. lights. the last. of the grasses.
long shadows. spill sideways. even at noon.
blue bruises. pool. in shade shallows.
air bubbles. under thin. ice. skin.

OF WATCHES

time exceeds language.
face and hands are words
borrowed from the body.

watch, a word for vigilance.
pocket, a soft absence.
time, a frame.

in the present tense we wind up
using the same word as wind,
a general disturbance of air.

in the past, tense.
keyed up.
tightly wound.

a ticking time.
does not heal all.
we use the word to wound.

OF TIME

for Barbara Catalani

One hand holds the exhaustion.
Working. Away. In a suburb of Rome.
Between two televisions, blaring.
Three languages. Four deadlines.
A long waiting. No trains.
Will this flight cancel?
Feathers ruffle.
The arm aches to wing.

The other hand holds a cypress cone.
The ear, the sound of its falling.
Fresh. Green. And scheming.
I have interrupted something.
Walked in on. Walked on.
The cone at home now in my pocket.
Along with a small piece of marble.

One foot sorer than the other.
One foot in front of the other.
On a path of white pebbles.
In a columned portico.
One foot colossal, one toe chipped.
One foot in the past. One cast in plaster.
One for the mouth. One for the door.

Between a fragment and a figment.
One can only speculate.
This is a hard place to concentrate.
When in Rome.
If a Roman invites you
somewhere, you go.
Between lunch and dinner.
Between antiquity and a roundabout.
A side street is being resurfaced.

In the Protestant Cemetery.
Today. I saw an actual pomegranate.
For the first time. I mean, alive.
Growing from what I can only presume
to be an actual pomegranate tree.
And then I heard the cypress cone fall.
And then I found it. And then I held it.

What I'm trying to say is,
I don't have time.

Time has me.

OF SWIFT

after Percy Bysshe Shelley

O uncontrollable! throughs of rain and
flowers, sea-blooms and towers. living hues.
the horizon sudden pale, and hectic red.

unextinguished locks of rain, shook from head.
and summer lightning, quivering, O hear!
tameless, O Wind! over unseen presence.

uplift me as a wave, as a hill burst.
the height of your voice, the breath of your air.
oozy woods, wakened moss, sky head, and hair.

what if my leaves saw through this commotion.
swift cloud! if I were a swift cloud! loose cloud
or winged seeds spread on solid atmosphere.

on bay, on bright, O sister of ocean!
lay your azure head, lulled by incantation
by this crystalline stream, summer dreaming

of vapours from the Atlantic. O hear!
the tangled boughs of leaves, and of forest
overgrown with sweet buds. mid the bright air.

O hear! my lips quicken to multitudes
like flocks to feed. beneath the blue surface
a deep, autumnal tone. scatter, you dirge.

the dim verge and tremble of an isle
comrade of a vast sky, vaulted with cold.
might I with you, in all your wanderings

OF DRIP

    after T. S. Eliot

in this only year. broken. by river. blind.
through waiting. beating oars. I come burning.

wet bank. damp gust. look! I'm glass. and pearls.
drip drop drop drip drop drowned. I sail, and down.

in empty rooms, I lurk houses. count mountains.
and tall the silence. tall as you. sweet you. I glad beside you.

I once was breasts. exploring hands. under camisoles.
her hair wet, I last was rain. drip drop drop falling.

dry grass singing. I shall something. la la la burning.
turning. wide, to folly. she sun beats, to wings.

we ships, thank you. shore eyes. and fear. in careful.
flushed and tired. we suffered. under ceiling.

my nerves. your shakings. drip drop drop noise.
upon the garden. this stony rubbish. will it bloom?

I do not nothing. I could not silence.
chatter fool, I speak not loud. I sailor, too.

and home from sea. swallow swallow.
these fragments. cracked hours.

but O O the moon. she turn in moonlight.
a moment so elegant. she turning.

and I singing drip drop. and if gliding.
wind crossing. bright. under bone.

OF DOUBLES

how the river finds me. ribbons me.
green sinews. and shallows me.
nestles we. in chalk bed.

how I am willow. brushing surface.
a sway thing. invasive.
blooming. in squelch shade.

how the river doubles me.
and all around me. there rustles we.
grass golden. seed. and heat.

and how the river. is also vertical.
ribboning up. from said chalk bed.
green light. and rush sound.

leaping. from shallow. shade surface.
to willow me. I shiver curtain.
of quivering leaf.

OF DROUGHT

what tricks play. on the heart mind.
to shuffle. through leaves burnt.

orange. fallen. in mid-August.
grass bare. beyond the shade.

glare. under high dry. blue sky.
oxeye. open. and waiting.

what tricks the body. thin skin.
breathing. in a longing. slow ageing.

wakes a nosebleed. in a barely breeze.
a mucus membrane. cracks open.

how cloud we. into sky pond.
how owl shape. into hollow tree.

how limb bend. this elbow branch.
and how also. how lichen. how knee.

dry grasses. glimmer wet. after rain. but say:
we became drought. and now we are golden.

and nobody. not even the rain.
has such small hands.

how mysterious. the sudden appearance.
of this floating. jaggy lightening.

lines of bright. at the edge of vision.
an impairment. or an apparition.

       I'm not after an explanation.

for how the slant light. in the old cemetery.
picks and chooses. what to bright.

when to distance. where to skew.
how to dust. and rest fallen angels.

how the heat came. morning. soaking. into body.
how the sweat came. dripping. salt. into eye.

and we became island. sand. between toes.
until we went. evening. striding. into long sea.

shallow. as skin. some distant. wind.
swelling waves. stirring. underthings.

I live here now. in sunburn. and salt hair.
an island. pinned to haze horizon.

I split double. part shimmer.
part cinder. of drought.

OF LAMENT

after Jules Laforgue

another Sunday.
cut out of October.

a window of wind.
drawn blind.

on bald landscape.
poorly constructed.

the livid sunset.
a seeping wound.

corners a room.
hung with stockings.

bare legs.
long dry.

five trees.
in petty gusts.

the raw sky.
marbled.

with bandages.
wisteria bones.

bound with strings.
lace straps.

wedding morning.
wood curling.

an agony.
worms.

sordid slugs.
under this suit.

this endless room.
and then after.

a landscape.
very wind.

OF WIND

What is the wind?

    A force in the bodies of living things?

What is its origin?

    Low marshy districts?

How is it formed?

    By the gradual collection
    of small quantities
    of exhalation?

How does it arise?

    Encouraged by sun?

What are its motives?

    To sweep clouds along
    with a great noise
    close to the earth?

And what are we to suppose its nature to be?

    Portent of some greater catastrophe?

Are we to suppose that the wind flows
like a stream from some vessel?

> And continues to flow
> until the vessel is empty?

Or are the winds self-originating,
as the painters depict them?

> Is it absurd to suppose that the air which surrounds us becomes wind simply by being in motion?

How do we drag ourselves out of the classical period?

> On horses. Winged chariots. Wings attached to shoulders, or sandals. Signifying speed.

Sailing. Into the early-modern.

> Our ships no stronger than a nutshell.

Under a press of sail.

> Wind resists the sail. Scours the sea.

Carries off moisture.

> Carries off bodies. Heaps up white foam.

Whitecaps everywhere.

> Reefed jib. Topsails struck.

A plague upon this howling.

> Woe to any ship embroiled in this hurly-burly.

For most of human history
the ship was the fastest we could travel.

    The furthest we could think.

Wind was the invisible force
powering colonial expansion.

    The *volta do mar,* the turn of the sea.

Winds prevailing easterly.

    Trading oceans for islands.

Icebergs for spice routes.

    Whalebones for corsets.

Wool blankets for hats of finest beaver felt.

Data from the log books of wind-powered sailing ships
continues to inform our daily thoughts and actions.

    When we check the weather app on our phones, we
    send old winds rattling round the Cray XC40
    supercomputing system at the Met Office.

Whispers to the sail.

    Breezes. Eddying around ankles.

Skirts, cloaks, hair, welling with air.

    Wind in the teeth. Of a gale.

How do we evoke through the materiality of language an invisible force such as wind which we can only perceive indirectly, through its affect?

    Prayer flags flapping.

Soap bubbles drifting.

    Rose petals falling.

High moorland hawthorn.

    Grown blown sideways.

A body of dry exhalation.

    An inconvenience felt in walking.

What is writing anyway?

    Wind writes texts which are read with difficulty.

Umbrellas are used with difficulty.

    Smoke rises vertically.

Crested wavelets form on inland waters.

    A trace on the face, felt but not seen,
    requires a transformational reading regime.

We order our days and months into an arbitrary gird.

    Wind rushes through this rational structure.

Leaving behind a residue.

    Of fallen leaves.

Tumbleweeds.

    Plastic bags tangled in trees.

Unwriterly texts.

    Unpublishable.

At Gale Force 8, wind lifts spray off cresting waves.

    Spindrift, it's called, in southern England.

And what if we are inland?

    In Scotland. The synonymous word, spoondrift,
    may also be used for fine snow blown off hilltops.

And what if we are endeavouring to shed
the linguistic cloak of colonialism?

    Walking. In winter. In amiskwacîwâskahikan.
    In Treaty 6 Territory. old woman bear teaches me:
    papêskwacistin, a Plains Cree word meaning a wave
    of snow drifting across the rest of the snow.

And what if we are birds?

    Are we part of weather?

What if there are so many ravens in the sky that a dark cloud
forms in the shape of a raven over the horizon?

    Then we are kamâmawipayitwaw pîwâyisak,
    a wave of birds flying together.

And what if the wind stops, for one damn minute,
stops speaking, creaking, cracking, groaning, moaning,
screaming, screeching, howling?

> Then we might hear pitihkwêkâstan,
> the sound of wings unfolding,
> feathers rustling.

And what if we are born of wind-borne pollen?

> This is called anemophily, by science.

This is called sex, by grasses, sedges, and rushes. Wheat, rice, corn, rye, barley, and oats. Pines, spruces, firs, alders, aspen, poplars, and certain hardwoods.

> Large branches in motion.

Whole trees in motion.

> It rains slates and tiles in the town
> and there is no standing on the beach.

And what if we are walking on the beach?

> Must our mouths be cold?

Mist on the sea.

> Advancing.

A salty tang of brine
commonly enters our mouth.

OF WITCHES

after Barbara Reti

well, I did hear a story
there was an old woman
(I don't want to mention her name)

a kin-less old woman
(not named in the story)
a hard ticket, a dark complexion
(she never bothered us none)
tiny, with a bun of white hair

she was the bold type
she'd go around the houses
attended by her black crackie
(even though dogs weren't allowed in the community)

everybody gave her what she asked for
(they wouldn't dare say no)

everything she said would happen, did happen
her words had an instant, transforming effect

you'll be sorry for that by the end of the month
you'll be sorry before fall

she meandered along in her battered brown coat
eating snow from the side of the road

she wandered and talked in circles

you won't be getting me this time
you won't be feeling so well

she became sick
(ask anybody home now)

the birds were never so thick
the birds came close to the beaches

a giant bird was seen to pass eastward
black under the wing and therefore inedible

a crow came right down there by the window
(I didn't say anything to anybody)

there was always a black crow following the boat
several boats ran aground the summer after
(piece that together to suit yourself)

there were little whispers, currents of malice
scant details, ambiguous words

hissing, heavy breathing
swishing, as of cloth, and guttural voices

spirits like misty horses rush into the room
a dream that something is going to kill you

you won't reach harbour this night
you won't sleep right again

she come right up on her, she come up on her,
and she had her down, and she couldn't move,
she couldn't even speak, only she was there,
you know, trying to get her breath

don't mess with her, she'll tie you up in knots
(that's what you're made to believe)

a dark, sly look
(she put a spell on him, see?)

you'll never shoot another goose

the geese began to die, one by one

you won't get a fish
you won't get nar one

no fish, no fish, no work and no fish
dire prediction dashed along with the dishes

you'll have more trouble than that, too

there wasn't one person had a bite to eat
(as everyone knew)

you can put your nets out now

the fish return to normal in colour

you'll have a good season now

just like that the fish come back
(as true as the sun my dear)

the waves calm around them
(yes my dear, you can count on it)

you'll be alright in a little while
you'll be better in a day or two

(better treat her good, else)

you'll pay
you'll die
you dirt
you blood of a bitch

                                                that's all, that's all
                                                  there's nobody
                                                  knows her today

OF DEW

after William Charles Wells

bodies in contact with the atmosphere
observed on still and serene nights
readily precipitate dew

bodies in among other bodies
similarly situated in open air
copiously attract dew

other bodies of the same kind
equally exposed to the night air
also exposed to the sky

with various other bodies
similarly exposed bodies
similarly exposed to the sky

what is the real temperature
of bodies of a different nature
in similar circumstances

of bodies a little elevated
and similar bodies
lying on the ground

sometimes bodies
having smooth surfaces
become colder than the air

at night, bodies on the ground receive little heat
from the lower surface of other bodies
more attractive of dew

on other nights, bodies thus situated
will be less dewed on their upper surface
than other solid bodies

between the temperature of these bodies
the surfaces of these bodies
the tendencies of various bodies

the mechanical state of bodies
the chemical form of bodies
the incapacity of bodies

of all bodies indiscriminately
bodies which conduct electricity
bodies which attract dew

among the bodies of this class
inferior to the bodies of the first class
solid bodies are more cooled

only a small part of bodies in contact
with all the bodies just mentioned
will refuse in a similar way

bodies in the state of a powder
having a surface exposed to the influence
of other bodies warmer than themselves

bodies situated on or near the surface
between bodies lying on the grass
and the atmosphere near to it

bodies become colder than the neighbouring air
respecting the communication of heat
the nightly radiation of heat

among bodies lying in the open air
bodies lying with other bodies
of the same temperature

the moon communicates moisture
to bodies exposed to its light
exposed in a clear night

in such a state of things
bodies condense rising vapour
replete with moisture

respecting the difference
in the capacities of bodies
all bodies will become moist

in such a situation
subject to a cloudy sky
as I have formerly shown

when bodies become cold
bodies must grow colder
if only a little colder

the hurtful effects of cold
occur chiefly in hollow places
as far as I know

I have never perceived dew
on any naked part
of my own body

though my attention was much occupied
with everything relative
to this fluid

for a three-year period
my body was much exposed
to cold night air

OF AIR

   after Robert Boyle

what we understand by the air

     that thin, fluid, diaphanous body
     in which we breathe
     wherein we move

the constant and permanent ingredients of the air

     that numberless multitude of vapours
               of exceedingly
                    minute parts
     innumerable particles   of what we call light
     elastic particles like springs of watches
          slender wires
          curled hairs of wool
          thin shavings of wood

the destruction, generation, and absorption of the air

     necessary to the well-being
          the very being
              being a body

     notwithstanding the difficulties
     I desire to be understood in a familiar sense

the moisture and dryness of the air

    a body is dry
    a quality near of kin a privation may occasion
    a change of texture

of mists

    a blue-ish mist ascends
    from a ground moist   in winter
    and then subsides again in dew

of terrestrial steams

    pillars of fumes and fogs
    ascending like smoke
    some inodorous
        ill-scented
        lasting
        of large spread
    require no tender nostril
    to perceive them to stink

of lightning

    a strong odour of burnt brimstone
    there did fall something
    the strangest   thing
    yet to be mentioned

of the air as medium of sounds

       the sky is of a sudden black
                            thick
       breaking forth on every side
       rattling continually
       incessantly flashing
       enough to amaze the resolute
       most accustomed to the noise

of the motion of the air and of winds

    a dreadful storm
    so exceedingly violent
    nothing could stand before it
    carried beasts into the sea

    houses ruined
         laid flat
            exceedingly shattered

    no place could keep persons
                      books
                      papers
    free from wind
           rain

    hourly we feared the falling
    of the fort
         wall of the town

    yet abroad
    we could have no shelter

of the heat and coldness of the air

    it's obvious to every sense
    the summer heat has manifest effects
    upon easily agitable bodies
        the juices and flesh of animals
        the softer parts of vegetables
    but that even in places sheltered from the sun
    the warmth of a temperate summer
    should be able to expand so cold a body as glass
    would not be easily believed

of the air in reference to light

    one day
    walking the beach
    to enjoy the fresh air
            prospect of the sea
    casually
    looking forwards
    to the verge of the visible horizon
    discovered there a new coast
    rising and falling

    grounds emerged out of the ocean
    in a place where no such thing
    had been seen before

    after it had been gazed upon
    this delightful spectacle
    did slowly disappear

of the air in reference to fire and flame

      about the burning of candles
      the depths I desired to be informed of
      were very uncertain and varied considerably

of the operation of the air on the odours of animal substances

      it was difficult to discern in the morning
      any peculiar smell of what had been cast
      into the street the night before
      dogs lay dead
      deprived of stench

of the operation of the air on the colours of animal substances

      there is a region where white people
      do in a very short time grow tawny

      flocks of certain birds are white in the winter
                                    grey in the summer

of the operation of the air on the colours of mineral substances

      solid stones
      change their colour oddly

      in a large piece of ground
      newly under tillage
                      rust-coloured
      afterwards   lighter coloured
      after four years white

of the operation of the air on the colours of
vegetable substances

      trees
      when newly cut down
      will quickly green
      though that beneath
      be yellow

of the air introducing other less obvious qualities into
vegetable substances

      great heat and moisture
      despoils bodies
                  finds
      white sugar full of maggots
      ointments verminous
                  brings
      sweet-meats to putrefy

      air too dry
      is not favourable
      for the production of insects
      no soft garden snails
      for want of moist vapours
      few fleas in the house

of the air in reference to the propagation of plants

      observe
      a scarce credible difference
      between the sides of mountains

        one side verdant and flourishing
            yielded a delightful prospect
                plentiful provisions

the other side parched
        russet
        barren
        dismal
        a wilderness
        blasted by winds

of the air in reference to the life and health of animals

    mere local motion
    should be mentioned
    as it may operate on other bodies

    perhaps among the more tender sort of animals
    there may be found some in which the motion
    of external air may have considerable operation

of heavy bodies sustained or taken up into the air

of dew

of rain

of hail

of snow

of other things falling out of the air

promiscuous experiments and observation of the air

desiderata in the history of the air

and proposals for supplying them

OF WEST

with questions from Mary Paterson

Which way is west?

    Where is the ocean in relation
    to the moving body.
    To the migrant.

    Where once was land
    now low sun sets
    into vast water.

How slow is a curve?

    The delayed train
    slows its way
    around the wide bay.

How many places are there in your name?

    No places.
    A name displaces.
    A word before a body.

    After a great-aunt.
    By a father who left.
    His mother a ghost neighbour.

    His widow a side-step.
    After the facts.
    After the math.

    What is the name
    for a great half step
    queer fracture?

What will you leave behind?

    An archive.
    Of half-truth versions.
    Draft fragments.

    Files folders failures.
    The bay as the train slows onwards.
    The notion that west is landward.

What are you waiting for?

    Something recognizable.
    Something familiar,
    to hold against so much newness.

    A sense.
    Of belonging.
    Of home.

    Quiet.
    An open-ended structure.
    Within which to…

When are you going to slow down?

When will it feel safe to?
When belonging happens?
When quiet commences?

When sun setting not rising
setting over vast water
starts to feel normal?

How fast is a line?

    The train slows its way along a line of coast.
    On course.
    But not on time.

    Of course,
    the body slows with it.
    But the mind races ahead.

    Along lines of flight,
    of code, of memory,
    of poetry, of inquiry.

Who is missing you?

    This we can never know.
    The shape we make in the mind of another.
    A lover missing the point, tone, intonation.

    Is no longer loving listening.
    A mother who does not will cannot say,
    and so creates an absence.

Years of missing
messing with me.
Who is missing in me?

What is a trip hazard?

    Trip up off.
    A slip of.
    The tongue twist.

    Too left.
    Feet seem the least of it.
    A pre-occupational hazard.

    The delay.
    The train.
    The curve.

    The bay.
    The displacement.
    The half step queer fracture.

Where is the base line?

    The tide goes out and keeps going.
    Horizon line as far as eye can sea.
    And still the waters.

    The tide comes in again and keeps coming.
    Over the sea wall.
    Over the train line.

The cliff face falls.
Red in the.
Wide bay eats its way.

Into.
Strata.
Of Triassic sandstone.

Where solid meets sand.
Where the now sea.
Meets the once desert.

What is beyond your body?

> The spoken word escapes the body as breath and immediately it is captured. Thing-like it hangs frozen in the air on a cold morning, carves a path on a wax cylinder, wakes waves on water, displays green peaks and valleys on digital monitors, tickles the *stereocilia* of another body. Spiralling toward an inner ear, the spoken word becomes part body again — mingling air, hair, fluid, and flesh.

What is off the scale?

> What, in its scant imperceptible inchoate unpleasant uncertain unstable abject insistence, consistently evades register?

> The whisper. The gesture.
> The glance. The gaze.
> Longing.

The scales.
Fall from our eyes.

What is too small to be seen?

A moment.
A movement.
A process occurring with the spectrum of the already invisible.

A change of temperature.
A quickening of pace of pulse of breath of wind.
An electrical current.

A flea in the dark
can be as hard to see
as a circus elephant.

What is traceable from above?

Where does above start?

With the wind blowing above the ocean's currents flowing above Tectonic plates floating above liquid magma encircling the Earth's molten core?

With our planet's orbit around the sun?

With the sun's slow arc in a dark galaxy still unfolding its incomprehensibly ancient wings?

What is triangulating your data?

The Home Away From
Office has my fingerprints.

The dog knows the sound
of my computer shutting down.

My phone suggests
a shorter route.

Who is watching?

The fox who lives in the wood beyond the back
garden has been twice now been startled to find me
quietly reading.

The women who work at the Post Office have noted
my recent purchase of brightly coloured envelopes.

My downstairs neighbour says she only ever sees me
in the rain.

Who is practising?

Our lips move.
Practising silent speeches.
Arguments knock about in our heads.

Who is prevented from being here?

The unaffiliated.
The un-abled to pay the train un-fair.
To navigate the stair un-well.

> The full-time worker
> carer child minder.
> The zero hours.
> Contact her.
> The aforementioned
> great half step queer.
> The lover.
> The mother.
> The missing.
>
> Are you too poor
> to fall in love
> with a foreigner?

Who wins in this scenario?

> Could it not be
> about winning,
> please,
> just this once?

What is happening in public?

> Walking, whiling, working away.
> Money, memory, meaning making.
> Space, time, train taking (a slow curve).

What is a suspicious activity?

> Speaking. Up. Out. Back.
> A foreign language.
> Reading.

    Writing.
    Migrating.
    Dining alone.

What is a territory?

    Childhood.
    Friendship.
    Family.

    Marriage.
    Memory.
    A shared language bed.

What is an empire?

    An uncommon wealth.
    An uncivil service.
    A paper work.

    A paper trail.
    An accidental accent.
    A tongue not my mother's rivers in my mouth.

What is a privilege?

    Not having to ask this question.
    Not being asked this question.
    Not answering this question.
    Not questioning.

What is left to the last minute?

> Inaction is an action.
> Indecision is a decision.
> The last minute is a hostage situation.

What is left to be seen?

> The erratic after the glacier.
> The dew after the night's cool.
> The short after the list.
>
> The tourists after the ruins.
> The sound after the wave.
> The wave after the shore.
>
> The time of arrival
> after the delayed train.

OF WHERE?

with questions from Mary Paterson

Where does the wind go?

How does the tide take?

Why does the time lean?

How does the mist steam?

Why does the land loose?

Where does the end come?

Where do we up-end?

How do we crumble?

Where are we accidental?

When do we hold?

What do we hunger?

Where did we leave home?

Have the days always been so short?

Have the nights ever been this bright?

Have the winters always been so dry?

Have the mornings ever been this windy?

Have the evening skies always been so massive?

Have the night skies ever been this empty?

Have the summer skies always been so hazy?

Are birds not part of weather?

Are feathers not also weather?

Are shadows considered weather?

Are demons sometimes weather?

Are flowers not part of sunshine?

Are swallows not part of wind?

Are seeds also part of wind?

How do seeds avoid the gaps between islands?

How do ships measure the distance between silences?

How do gulls avoid the static between ships?

How do sailors describe the absence between ports?

How do historians read the interval between gusts?

How do flowers annotate the distance between droughts?

How do bears occupy the space between rain drops?

How many raindrops fell here last year?

How many snowflakes fell in this country this morning?

How many dust motes fell on this island this season?

How many hours fell in this ocean this waiting?

How many breezes in your hair this wanting?

How many gusts in this storm this howling?

How many breaths in your silence?

remember silence?

remember seasons?

remember whale songs?

remember glaciers?

remember gentle breezes?

remember soft touches?

remember whispers?

remember mist?

remember joy?

remember ease?

OF NOTHING

after John Cage

I am here. and there is nothing to say. no whispering. wind in the wych elm. no rumour. of rain. in the river even. the water a rush of nothing I know the language for. and on the far shore. a loose assortment of nothing I know the name of. if among you there is a wish to get somewhere. you may wish. to leave at any moment. if among you there is a murmur. of morning mist. of stone cold. silences. fingers red. and fossilised corals. frozen in time. what cold requires is. that I leave off lecturing. what stone requires is. that that I go on walking. push over a boulder. and the pushed reveals another. an entertainment of the relative significance of marine fossils found in bedrock. as opposed to marine fossils found in cobble. a discussion of the relative knowing of birds identified by song. as opposed to birds identified by sight. I am not opposed to not seeing. song is not silent. even if we are not speaking. stones are not nothing. even if not ocean. and we are now crawling. squint. over cobble covered with sun-cracked. silt. dry creates an absence. nothing produces a surface. and speaks some other language. shall we discuss this later? measure. this whether. we simply decide. the names for these marvels. or agree. to none. to put no name. to know no thing. to refuse. to organise. to lecture on. or in. this space between rain drops. of time between lightning strikes. lecture on whatever you like. there are silences we want to do away with. there are stones that help make silences sink. into nothing. there are silences that let stones think. attach to any one stone any one thought. it falls down easily. I have nothing to say. and I am saying it. and that is poetry. as I need it.

OF SOURCES

Roland Barthes, *The Pleasure of the Text.* 1975.

Charles-François Beautemps-Beaupré, *An Introduction to the Practice of Nautical Surveying,* Richard Copeland trans. 1823

Robert Boyle, *A General History of the Air.* 1692.

John Cage, *Silence: Lectures & Wiring.* 1961.

Margaret Cavendish, *Observations Upon Experimental Philosophy.* 1668.

T. S. Eliot, *The Waste Land.* 1922.

Robert Hooke, *Micrographia.* 1665.

Jean Giraudoux, *Suzanne and the Pacific.* 1921.

Caroline Herschel, *An Account of a New Comet.* Read at the Royal Society, November 9, 1786

Barbara Reti, *Making Witches.* 2008.

Percy Bysshe Shelley, *Ode to the West Wind.* 1820.

William Charles Wells, *An Essay on Dew, And Several Appearances Connected with It.* 1838.

OF THANKS

This writing was made possible by financial support from Canada Council for the Arts and AHRC- and DFG-funded Research Fellowship at the University of Southampton.

Some of these poems have previously appeared, often in other forms and/or by other names, in: *above/ground, All Keyboards are Legitimate, The Capilano Review, Chicago Review, Futch, Here + There (The Wasteland), Lune: A Journal of Literary Misrule, The Pleasure of the Coast, PRISM International, Something Other,* and *Words of Weather: A Glossary.* Thanks to all the readers and editors who have invited, encouraged, and helped to shape and share this work.

Special thanks to Jordan Abel, old woman bear, Barbara Catalani, Heather Collins, Maddy Costa, Susannah V. Evans, Nathan Jones, Larissa Lai, Rob McLennan, Ghazal Mosadeq, Marilène Oliver, Jussi Parikka, Mary Paterson, Shazia Hafiz Ramji, Arnaud Regnauld, Lisa Robertson, and Judith Willson.

www.ingramcontent.com/pod-product-compliance
Ingram Content Group UK Ltd.
Pitfield, Milton Keynes, MK11 3LW, UK
UKHW040639180225
455202UK00001B/100